An Observer's Book of Birds

Published by Felin Press

Jon James was born in 1958 in Northampton. After taking an Art Foundation course he worked as a jeweller for some years before becoming interested in science. Subsequent years were spent interleaving studying physics at the University of East Anglia, Reading University and The Open University with working on numerical weather prediction and climate modelling at the Meteorological Office and on engineering applications of physics at The Open University.

D1740347

An Observer's Book of Birds

Poems and Sketches

Jon James

First published by Felin Press in 2018

ISBN 978-1-9993590-0-3

FELIN
PRESS

Thanks to Andrew James for assistance with editing and production advice and to Richard James for design and layout.

Cover design: Richard James, Jon James

For family and friends

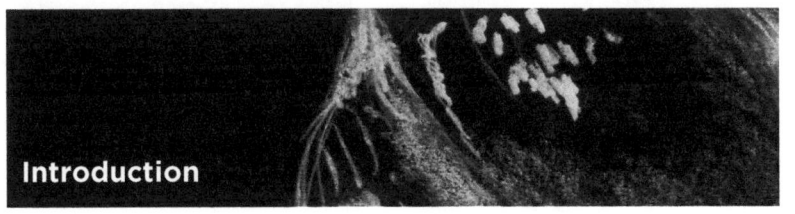

Introduction

A small collection of written and drawn sketches around the theme of birds. Sometimes the birds are the main subject and sometimes they are an element in the landscape. The sketches were, in most cases, inspired by sightings or observations and for want of any other system I have grouped them according to the regions of the country in which they occurred: Scotland, Norfolk and the east coast, Pembrokeshire and that area of the Oxfordshire-Northamptonshire-Warwickshire border known as 'Banburyshire'.

Scotland

Scotland. What to say? To borrow a phrase from author Adam Nicolson, 'the longed-for place' and a special destination for over fifty years.

Early holidays were to the Ardnamurchan peninsula, far up on the west coast. Just to get there was a two-day adventure. Now it seems you have to go just that bit further for the same feeling of isolation and peace, and so the Outer Hebrides are favoured.

Birdwatching started for me in Scotland. Looking out for exotic species such as buzzards, dippers, wheatears or maybe a black-throated or red-throated diver in 'The Bay'[1], the more common and less dramatic species, such as pipits, were, if anything, an irritation. But strangely it is the pipits that kept cropping up in these sketches.

[1] Swordle Bay, Ardnamurchan.

By-catch (a true story)

Pipits, trapped in lobster pots, stacked against the old

pier wall.

Release was easy,

a simple plastic latch

and they were gone;

with all the thanks and backward glances of a child

leaving home.

But nothing would I ask for this gift of freedom,

except maybe catch their feet as they fly,

and so spend another day

among the shoreline rocks and the long grass of

the machair[1].

[1.]*Fertile coastal plain, often carpeted in wild flowers.*

Eoligarry Pier

Eoligarry.

The north end of the island.

Where, last year, we watched the godwits feed.

Stone arms flung into wide heaven.

Water, clear as a solved riddle.

Skye 2013

There is no trauma of war

to keep me from my Blue Remembered Hills[1].

They are there now;

through the open car window.

The hills that mean so much.

And there, look!

flying in front,

a small flock of pipits

plays tag with the car

for a fence post or two;

before scattering

into the country on either side.

(Just as they ever did.)

And later,

in front of the tent,

the holy of holies,

the contraption,

dirty black vestments,

anointing with oils,

the vital spark, (the sprat to catch a mackerel),

Primus stove[2],

time machine.

[1.]*Reference to A. E. Housman's poem 'Into my heart an air that kills'*
[2.]*A paraffin camping stove, much beloved by my late father for 'brewing up'.*

Cormorant

Cormorant.

Wellsian time traveller.

Stationary as the aeons flicker past.

But having no candle,

and being careless of fashion,

his only measure of time,

the slow black wave-wearing of the rocks.

Scottish Single-track Road

Memories flushed out by the car,

fly in front,

like a flock of pipits;

nearby for a while,

then scattering

to the hills on either side.

Too distant to tell meadow from rock[1].

Too close to tell thought from feeling.

[1.] *Meadow pipits and rock pipits are visually very similar.*

Cormorant II (A 'Just-so' story)

The cormorant used to produce oil to waterproof its

wings when preening,

but it began to see this as signifying a rather unbecoming

level of activity

and engagement

which,

heaven forbid,

might be misconstrued

as attachment to the world.

So now,

when its wings are wet,

it just stands

with them open

on a rock in the sea,

and the wind,

(having no choice),

dries them.

And so honour is preserved,

and the wings get dry

soon enough.

Cormorant Juv. (field note)

It has been observed that some young cormorants

are defying what they describe as

the tyranny of biology

and are refusing to be born;

preferring to stay,

as smoother pebbles

on the shore.

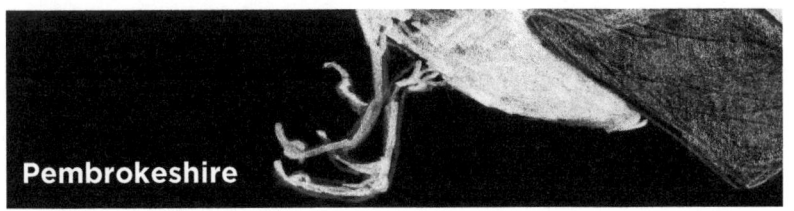

Pembrokeshire

The fact that Pembrokeshire (specifically the Pembrokeshire-Carmarthenshire border) is now 'home' is, for me, stark proof of the futility of trying to predict the future. I would never have thought I would end up living in Wales. The hills were just not the quite the right shape or colour, and anyway it just wasn't Scotland. Of course, it isn't Scotland, but it is a beautiful place nonetheless. The sea cliffs along the north coast are incomparable and the Preseli Hills have a feeling of wildness beyond their modest height. The juxtaposition of sea and hill and some subtlety of geometry creates a magical and powerful landscape.

The Pembrokeshire mainland is rich in wildlife and the islands of Skomer, Ramsey, Skokholm and Grassholm are home to colonies of puffins, gannets, razorbills, storm petrels and manx shearwaters.

Mynydd Preseli

An early frost;

white and sharp under a blue sky;

the air full of larks and the scent of sheep.

Grey rocks rise abruptly from winter-brown grass,

their surface lined and textured like elephant hide,

and with the same feeling of mass and warmth.

To have spent the night up here.

A clear dark sky, sliver Moon,

pin sharp Milky Way and Orion dipping toward the sea.

A night to have felt part of the Universe

and to have remembered.

Foel Drygarn

A short steep walk to the camp.

Windy, wild and lovely.

Smoke from heather-burning in the distance

lit sporadically as the sun found gaps in the cloud cover.

Then, coffee from a flask in the shelter of an outcrop.

Courting ravens riding a panicked wind

add to the wildness of the place.

Foel Drygarn - Raven detail

The claustrophobic wind,

trapped within the corrie,

panicked, shrieked,

and hurled itself toward

sky and escape.

The ravens,

uncaring,

rode the uprush,

diving, falling, tumbling

buoyant and laughing,

like corks in surf.

Starlings

A flash flood of starlings;

peaty and dark;

streamed over the rise

and down the wet hillside, leaving

droplets on the gate and fence. Then,

chattering and splashing against the rocks they dropped;

disappearing;

absorbed;

instantly;

into the already saturated ground.

Norfolk and the East Coast

Saltmarsh, mudflats and vast empty beaches; the east coast of the UK, particularly the North Norfolk Coast between Hunstanton and Cromer, has been a favourite destination for many years.

The habitats along this coast are of international importance; providing, amongst other things, wintering grounds for hundreds of thousands of geese and waders.

Lindisfarne Spring (for St Cuthbert)

Eye level with the pink bobbing sea thrift;

hunkered down among the bee-buzzed, sun-warm rocks;

safe, twixt wheeling sky and teeming sea,

the birds of the air,

gulls and kittiwakes,

build nests of weed, wind and grass,

and strangely,

here and there,

catching the sun,

catching the eye;

illuminated scraps,

Gospel fragments;

a monk's practice;

lofted high and across the islands -

a building material.

Summer Mooring

Not yet a leeward cove of some western isle;
rope trailing nightly cropped rabbit turf.

Nor bowline tied to a gneiss-driven ring
in orange, agate band of sea-loch bladder-wrack.

No.
For now, the other home.
The complementary pole.
The calm of Norfolk marsh and mud.
Dog walkers and a seafood van.
Broad sky, flint churches,
wind and tide.

And the boat.

One of a flock.

Long necks.

Clamouring halyards calling

(restless in the rising breeze).

Insistent.

Unnerving.

Like mugs against prison bars.

Gannets at Bempton

Clever apes lean out over the void

taking pictures of dinosaurs on smart phones.

Snettisham

Winter skeins pattern porcelain sky;

as tea-leaves around the rim after a swilled-out tide.

Banburyshire

A few years ago I spent a couple of hours most Saturday mornings walking the seven or so miles along the towpath of the Oxford Canal between Aynho Wharf and Banbury town centre; arriving in time for breakfast at Café Nero on the market square.

Not, you might expect, the most exciting or revelatory of walks, but some combination of internal and external lent it an unexpected significance and magic. The weather was mostly clear and fine and the wildlife rich. The list of sightings is too long to record here, but included swimming grass snakes and deer, a sparrowhawk, woodpeckers, chiffchaffs, reed warblers, reed buntings and, most memorably, swallows and kingfishers.

The Swallow

The gap is joined.

The spark flies.

The lock above the old bridge opens.

Summer floods.

The swallow has made the cut[1].

[1]Cut: another name for canal.

Motorway Cave

High in the Fingal-gloom

of the motorway cave

the common pigeons[1] sleep.

Lulled by the muffled crash and boom of the traffic surf;

the ebb and flow of human tide,

and dreaming dreams of west coast storms.

[1] *Pigeons are descended from rock doves that live and breed in sea caves along the west coast of the UK.*

Kingfisher

Potential sighting;

Static,

on a twig or branch,

for a moment or two,

before discharging

to bank or water,

then,

flowing off down the river-wire.

Swallow II

Low over the canal;

twisting, swooping, diving;

slender wings the colour of mussel shells or

summer twilight and,

under the chin,

a hint of summer warmth and of the

autumn to come.

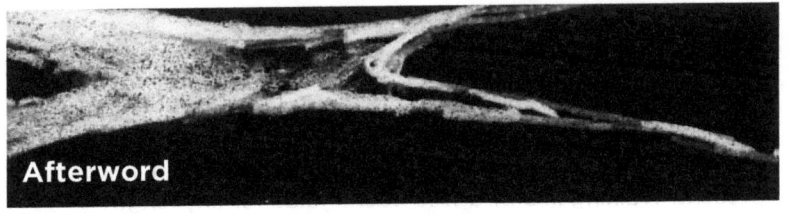

Afterword

Most of the sketches in this book were derived from photographs taken with a Nikon bridge camera. These cameras are a wonderful invention. For a couple of hundred pounds you have an almost pocket-sized camera with a zoom which allows you to take a picture of a whitethroat on a twig fifty yards away or capture the glint in the eye of a hovering kestrel.

When I first started bird watching as an eight or nine-year-old, I wanted to take photographs, but found that the sort of cameras available to me at the time reduced a bird to a tiny black spot at best. I tried various things, including attaching a pair of 8x30 binoculars to the front of my Instamatic; however, this failed, and I had to resort to blinking my eyes while simultaneously making a clicking noise with my tongue in imitation of taking a photograph and in the hope of committing an image to memory. Needless to say, although I remember the action of doing this, I don't remember any of the images I was trying to 'record'.

Of course, photographs taken with a bridge camera may not have the pin-sharp clarity of a top of the range 35mm SLR fitted with a powerful telephoto lens, but I am not really pursuing technical clarity in photography or, for that matter, in any other sense when it comes to bird watching. There are many ways to enjoy this pastime, from the intense to the casual and from the rational to the emotional and, having worked in science for many years, it is nice to take a softer, less rigorous approach to this pleasure and enjoy birds for their poetry and imagery.

Birds bring life to a landscape and are quickly missed if not present. Walking in a bird-free countryside for any length of time brings about a sort of creeping unease and sadness, followed by a powerful sense of relief when a flock, or even a flit, is seen. Unfortunately, while we have yet to experience Rachel Carson's Silent Spring, the news today is predominately of species decline due to pressures of habitat loss and climate change. Such news oppresses and saddens: we already have summers without cuckoos, do we also have to contemplate 'summers' without swallows?

There is an oft-quoted Chinese curse that runs: 'May you live in interesting times.'. The point, of course, being the irony that what should be the positive of living in interesting times is, in reality, a negative. Unfortunately, today it seems alternatives could easily be coined such as 'May you be born with a love of nature', or 'with an appreciation of wild places and wilderness.' Living in 2018 can be very uncomfortable if you care about any of these things.

On the other hand, there are good signs. The power of programs such as David Attenborough's 'Blue Planet' to raise public awareness of horrors such as the plastic pollution of the oceans is both impressive and heartening. Similarly, the BBC's 'Springwatch' has been hugely influential and effective in getting children interested in nature. A volunteer at RSPB Bempton told me recently that they attributed a three-fold increase in numbers and widening of the age range of visitors directly to this programme.